COMMON KNOWLEDGE:
CONTROLLING YOUR DESTINY

COMMON KNOWLEDGE:
CONTROLLING YOUR DESTINY

Beverly Bethea Griffin Shippy

Exposition Press
Hicksville, New York

ρ-85

To the woman who was my best friend, I dedicate this first book to you, my mother, the late great Vivian Holloman Griffin. May you forever rest in peace. And to my daddy, Ben D. Griffin, and my dear grandmother, Mrs. Birdie S. Holloman.

Contents

Acknowledgments

I would like to send out my sincerest thanks to my twin sister, Barbara, for her brilliant contribution to this work and my special thanks goes out to my baby sister, Benettye, who was also a great help. She kept my pencils sharpened and always ready for action. And most of all I would like to thank my husband James, whose patience and encouragement kept me going.

Preface

Many times people are not aware of the basic things they need to know about life, to reach their goals and to find inner happiness because everything seems to keep passing over their heads. Taking a little time out to indulge in some serious, concrete thinking about this very important matter will reshape your destiny and fulfill everything on earth you've ever wanted.

How many of you know for a fact that you have let many opportunities pass you by because you simply did not take advantage of them? There are record-breaking numbers of you out there, too, who have run into this knot of a problem and its consequences are extremely messy.

These problems do not come about because we are light, but because we do not always understand the opportunities that are open before us. We do not recognize these opportunities as hopes for rebirth but continuously pass them up, feeling either that they are impossible for us to reach, or worse, feeling that as the years pass by we will eventually reach this goal of ours somehow.

You also probably know, too, that everything you ever wanted could be yours and is very much within reach, if you know when and how to pursue it to the end. Once that's in order the last move is to commit yourself to the task. Knowing where you're going and how to get there is the common problem all of us face once in our lives; many people never find their dreams while living, and die miserable. Knowing where you're going and how to get there could mean all the difference in the world to your being much happier and living much longer.

Self-satisfaction is simple and should not be made complex by us in any form or fashion. Carefully analyzing your plans and temporary setbacks can make all the difference in the world in your final product and you personally.

Have you ever been so down and rejected that you felt like throwing in the dice because competition was too tough? Do you feel you have looked and looked at all possible alternatives and at this point, you are finally fed up! Well, for your information, every man and woman on earth has experienced this sometime in their lives, many several times, so you should know you are not alone. Somebody else out there is always worse off than you. But we all must cope. For many of us, rejection and depression is a daily routine that most of us never look forward to, but adjust internally when it's our turn to go through changes. Would you believe, some of us (look around you now because I may be hitting on your next-door neighbor) don't know what they're doing here, how they got here or where they're going. All they know is that they're here! Strange.

There are also some of you who feel you couldn't give your enemies the pleasure of seeing you set back, or failing. Actually, such feelings should make you stronger, make you push yourself harder to reach the top and stay there. The effort you use to get there, then the effort you use to stay there, will no doubt double but the interest will pay off well! Read *Common Knowledge*—then use yours.

Make that career decision final today. Then carefully initiate plans to follow through, which will lead directly to the goal you have in mind. The railroad train uses its engine to progress. You are much more fortunate, because you have a brain. Don't let the passing years dominate your train of thought, because one thing sure is, time will come and pass regardless of whether you make that move or not. Dwelling on time can deter the shrewdest of minds; you are persistent enough in your motives, you will gain considerably by those years rather than remain where you are now—stationary.

Whatever you do decide, remember it's your choice and nobody forced you. But wouldn't it be a lot more memorable to live through those years being where you want to be—finally, completely, happy and contented living a full, rich, life. (A rich life does not have to contain wealth.)

A must in this world is to know the make-up of your society which consists primarily of your environment, the people and their chemical and physical structures.

There are people who are emotional, timid and shy.

There are people who are bullies and considered a menace to society.

There are people who are indecisive, very suspicious and price-conscious.

Then there are people who shine out from all the rest in any group, like the rainbow that sets.

There are those of us who we know very well are nothing if not plain fools.

So since this make-up of groups may not be entirely new to you, I have included everybody, including you.

America is a land of opportunity. People don't plan to fail, they fail to plan!

COMMON KNOWLEDGE:
CONTROLLING YOUR DESTINY

God put us here on the intended terms no man is greater or better than the other but every man given a gift of determination and common knowledge to use or repress it as a tool to venture out into any phase he wants and challenges.

—BEVERLY BETHEA GRIFFIN SHIPPY

I

Positive Reinforcement Exercises

So the odds are against you, or at least you feel they are, anyhow. You're striving extra hard for that career move you want to make, but it looks like you may never make it. Well, for once in your life just stop whatever you're doing, right now and take a personal break to think awhile. No one ever made anything work unless he believed in himself first, then proceeded into his master plan of how to go about getting it, and then sticking to it.

After all those experiences you've lived through so far, you should already know that anything worth getting in life is worth working very hard toward. Nothing good comes too easy, and if it does, it can vanish with that same swiftness, leaving you still puzzled as to what just happened. It can disappear like quicksilver and even you may know this because it may have happened around you. Life's experiences never stop coming at you; they only reorganize themselves to recycle into another replay. From centuries too far back to document scientifically or accurately, the pharaohs practiced this brilliant technique as the secret to their rulership of great empires—determination, determination, determination.

Many of us just sit and waste many good years of our lives,

17

praying and hoping some god-sent miracle will come our way and sprinkle us with our most cherished hopes and dreams without much mental or physical force exerted. By not approaching these goals with consistent assertiveness and will power, the brain ceases to go through with its plans because the beginner force did not ignite the drive. Success then seems out of reach. By taking the all-out initiative to get what you always wanted out of your life, you would first of all have to keep pace with that goal or be miserable with yourself, hating your closest friend, the greatest person alive today—YOU!

The dream is there if you challenge it, if you want it. You see, it really doesn't matter what route you take to the top of anything. Some people take the stairway, which is tiresome but progressive. Some people go completely around the stairway making their journey a bit shorter than the stair climber. The sprinter goes straight up the middle, penetrating and progressing rapidly at light speed. This subject is aware of hidden obstacles that might be abstract and move unconditionally. So he must be alert to any interior motives because they are usually irrational and awkward.

You know, as large as this planet is, most people never take time out to think about the slots that are plentiful enough here to embrace every man, woman and child. Instead, we just sit back and take a nonchalant attitude about the whole thing, feeling it ain't for me to have. Any and everything on the face of this earth can be meant for you to have, but before you own this slot, you must know about a few things first. You've got to know what theory unlocks the chest to your stuffed piggy bank. You've got to know the combination to get inside. *YOU CANNOT BREAK IN!*

Now this could look very abstract to you but it shouldn't. All you have to do is prepare for it now, right now. No matter how old you are at this time, thoroughly analyze whatever job you may hold presently, giving it many hours of thought.

You may have to wait however until a weekend, if your job

and family responsibilties don't give you enough time to critically analyze it. Go off into your study room in your home or take a ride somewhere alone, but do go alone and think. Think of all the things you dislike in your present job, compare them with the good qualities related to your job and most likely you will come out with an imbalance. I don't have to tell you why, because you know better than I. You may not be satisfied and may not be able to pin down any one thing because everything is wrong, to the best of your knowledge. This can drive you plain disgusted and it doesn't have to be that way at all.

You know life can be extremely puzzling if you make it that way, and pretty damn exciting if you want it to be, but there is one thing that must accompany your pattern of success and that is guts. Guts to face the world, guts to reach your highest potential and follow up to hold your advancement after you've worked hard to get it. Guts—that's a shrewd word, isn't it, but it's a shrewd world, too, and only those people who exhibit this form of behavior occupy certain levels of superiority or wealth.

A real man deals with his feelings as they come to him. That is not a form of weakness but strength. At some point in your life, you probably worked your posterior off and still were only able to make ends meet.

The same way you got that job, you can get another one or better one, only if you take the time out to reorganize. Everybody needs reorganization no matter how organized they may appear to be. Every living soul needs room to rebuild and start all over again. This can range from the largest detail to the smallest reason. It's called reconstructing, reconstructing with the ultimate purpose of rebuilding yourself, your dream. Some jobs and some everyday situations are like baseball games—they only last nine innings.

It doesn't make much sense for any of us to live here on this earth and be unhappy with ourselves or our status in society. It's distasteful enough to have to be on constant guard against violence, not to mention going home after work everyday disgusted with yourself because you haven't progressed as fast as you think you should.

Give yourself a pat on the back. Go ahead and do it! Congratulate yourself several times, then after you finish put a big smile on your face and laugh. Get all that anxiety out of your system by laughing, or you may cry. Different strokes for different folks, but do it. There's no reason to be ashamed, because you're going to be alone anyway. Absolutely no one will see you, but after it's all over, you'll feel 100 percent better. Crying, laughing, jogging, flying, driving, swimming—people use different outlets for escapism. Which one will you choose or do you have a self-made method of your own? Whichever method you do use, you better believe it will definitely put you on the right track to finding yourself and your purpose in life.

Before you go any further, as of this moment, this hour, today, begin thinking positive and you can never go wrong. Congratulate yourself for the achievements you've made in your life so far and even if they do seem too small and irrelevant, you wouldn't have gotten that far had you not placed great confidence in yourself first. It happened then, it can happen again. Yes, it can happen to you, with your next leads becoming bigger and better pathways for you to grow in. Just like a flower sprouts out when it has reached its peak of growth, so will you. You will sprout out, then grow. Everybody who wants success will find success, because it's out there, waiting for you to take the challenge.

Go ahead, don't be afraid of what's happening around you. It's all for the better and will help you, in time, to grow into your goals, to grow better acquainted with yourself. But, if you don't want it, sit back and continue doing what you have been doing already—nothing. Your group is noncompetitive and you are quite satisfied with your codes and standards. You have no desire to climb. You're satisfied. Well now, that's O.K. too. All types of people make up this world and you are not alone. As a matter of fact, there are a couple of million of you out there who also share that same feeling. Look around you!

So when you wake up everyday dreading your position in life, angry because it is not where you want it to be, do something about it. Plan for your future. It's never too late for anything, except time. All good things come to an end if never pursued by you. So DON'T worry about the time because it goes and flies by like the birds in the sky. You just work within its tick and let the time take care of itself.

II

Paying Bills

Paying bills has become the American way of life. There's no way to escape them nor get around them. Everybody must pay dues then meet the yearly dues at the end of the year. Income tax.

An associate once told me after he finishes depositing his salary in his bank accounts, they swell so large they look like they are expecting, and after he pays out the bulk of it to creditors, it begins to look very undernourished—hungry, as a matter of fact. Everybody's got a hangup after those unwanted bills are met. Oddly enough, consumers begin paying dues at a very early age and this process continues until death, then some friend, relative or marriage partner may be left to take the load. Yes, those unwanted bills never stop coming. After the regular ones are paid up, new ones always blossom up somewhere to start that cycle all over again. For the fashion-conscious consumers, their bills usually stem from those wardrobe accounts. Loving clothes and how they look on you probably means a great deal to you, so that extra cash you may have will most likely go toward garments.

The holiday season is another time when the strain on the finances is tremendous. One season that especially creates a great amount of strain for consumers is Christmas. That gift list seems to never stop increasing. The more you try to cut your list down, the longer and longer it gets—you drop one name only to find out you missed another.

A friend once told me that after he finished with his Christmas list annually, even Saint Nicholas would want to tag a service charge for his time. The problem with my friend lies in his gift list, which involves increasing amounts of girl friends. But still he complains how hard it is for him to find a nice girl. As close as we are, he asks my advice as to how he could find that perfect lady. We've become very good friends through the years and correspond with each other often. Anyway, I suggested he stop splurging his money on so many women and try to slowly cut his list down to a few, then eventually, only one lady. Then I told him, friend, the rest is on you. I told him as long as he blows so much money on so many women, they would be almost crazy not to accept a gift from such an irresistible handsome man.

But what's so unpredictable about this man is that he never comes back. He took me into his confidence once and told me laughing . . . he gives out so many gifts, he forgets what gift he gave to whom. But one good thing about it, he said he never regretted was his income tax writeoff at the end of the year. He said he couldn't think of a better way to end out the year than to look forward to a collection from his hard-earned money. Well, all this time now, I was thinking in the back of my mind, that's why he hasn't got anybody. He doesn't try.

Oh, let's not forget how we bring in that new year, traditionally called New Year's Eve. Now the average person is drunk New Year's Eve before midnight anyway and since they're out on the town celebrating, cash is flowing through their hands so fast during these festivities, they could care less during those moments how much money they've already spent until the next day rolls around and their head has recovered.

Now this person hadn't planned on spending that much money but we are all aware of the fact that once too much of that liquor flows into your system, you're gone, it takes all control. Professional con artists find Christmas and New Year's their richest season because anything goes and so many innocent people get taken.

Anyway, after the splurge season is over, we all have headaches and regrets, using many choice words all over the place. But those bills must be paid! The two most historical times of the year turn out to be the most expensive. The secret to stopping them unfortunately is not available yet, since death and income tax are ultimately a part of your fate, but there is a helpful solution here that may be of interest to you as a word of advice. . . . Just live it and be thankful, happy and contented to be able to breathe, think, work, draw compensation, unemployment or welfare in this beautiful free land, because one thing for sure, those bills never stop coming!

I knew a friend once who went into a nationally known service station for a fill-up and a quart of oil which would have cost her $11.00, and ended up with a bill of $71.58. They charged her $60.00 and some change for a fan clutch. Of course this price did include parts and labor, how nice.

This happens every day on the road and people are continuously getting taken for unbelievable prices. These gas station people know you're in a hurry to be on your way so they tell you it'll only take fifteen to twenty minutes for them to correct your problem so you can get back on the road.

Well, those are the magic words—that time limit and a price you wouldn't be able to find anywhere within an hour from here. Now these figures they demand may not seem like profitable amounts, but you've got to figure when they pull four or five gigs like this a day, these gentlemen will pull in the average working man's monthly salary in one day and they still got six more good days to go. So you say, "O.K. I'll take it." This is an effective pattern they usually follow with that price slipping right on in there. Afterwards, you're highly disgusted as hell, but you were taken, you know that, so you jump back into your car and motor back up the highway saying to yourself, "Oh no, I just knew this could never have happened to me. I'm a sucker!"

Speaking of gas station ripoffs, a state trooper once pulled a job on a friend of mine once who attended college in Atlanta. He and his family were driving through a southern state from Connecticut on his way back for fall classes and were stopped in this southern state for speeding. My friend was driving at the time. The patrolman demanded $61.00 cash on the line immediately, stating his reason was for. . . . He blabbed on and on and on until he talked himself into a headache, my friend told me, the officer said, so his mother paid off the officer and was too happy it wasn't more money at the time, not caring or thinking too much at the immediate time about their mishap. The officer was sweating and so was my friend. They both went their separate ways.

So I had to tell my friend he had just been ripped off badly and he agreed. He told me laughing, he thought something wasn't right about paying the officer the money right there on the spot before going down to headquarters, but assumed that must have been a new southern law. Well he admitted they had been taken and pushed it off by saying, it happens to all good men at least once, anyway.

So as you continue living from day to day you run into some interesting things and situations. Take for instance the automobile industry which is one of the most fascinating businesses in operation today, with its manufacturing plants spread out in numerous countries around the world. Cars are big business which is one of the reasons they are so widely distributed and used all over the world.

The leading name brands on the market now are enough to discontinue production of any more new models for years to come and still run smoothly. Yet, they are still being built. Since car buyers have such a large line-up of cars to choose from today, the process is just as hideous and time consuming as shopping around for that new home. Why? You might say because both are considered investments.

A big part of car buying is also deciding on the type and price you feel will best suit your needs and budget. So, this process will take a large bit of thinking on your part. Naturally when you look for a car, the road performance will be high on your list of requirements. You also might consider your family size and the gas mileage this car can provide since gasoline prices are beginning to rise sky high. All these factors consumers look into before they buy that next investment called the automobile. But, once you make that decision no one can change that mind of yours. It's final. Now a year or so has passed since you invested in your car and you're now looking for another car as a treasure piece to add to your collection or desperately needing another one immediately because your present car took sick and expired, costing you more money right now than you'll be willing to pay.

Many cars, like people, live short life careers, so be prepared, car buyers, to spend lavishly in the automobile industry. Although some cars exhibit longer durability and the warranty may stretch a little longer, by the time you wait for a part to come from across the ocean, through a couple of states and finally to your problem, your head will probably be hurting from that long wait, and you have probably put dozens of people to a disadvantage as far as catching a ride here and there is concerned and you are by now just plain disgusted and/or frustrated.

Yes, car buyers today are caught up in a whirl of one of the richest businesses in America today. Everybody needs one. Although in the larger metropolitan cities where you have convenient transit lines involving your subway, trains and public transportation, everybody still wants a car to own or call their own.

The automobile industry will always survive because like many products sold here in the United States and other countries of the world, automobiles are one of the products that will never lose ground. They're as much a necessity as shelter, especially if you live in the suburbs or rural areas where public transportation is seldom available into the city every five to ten minutes during rush hour. So a car is the next best thing to making sure you get there.

America is a country that stresses only the best so you will see that future cars will be smaller and include the same luxury accessories the larger cars have to offer. Maybe with a little luck your final choice will be a sure bargain in your favor which you thrive on very strongly.

Now there still will be larger cars to purchase but the industry is beginning to produce the smaller cars gradually since the manufacturers and the oil companies can't seem to get together on this thing. However, the industry will still make available to consumers the larger luxury cars that eat up gas to just crank up. I presume their owners don't feed them enough but such owners of these gas guzzlers may not mind that disadvantage. Their money is healthy and consistent so they don't mind at all spending big money on an automobile. The price fits so they buy. Nothing wrong with that providing you aren't starving—America is a country that wants to keep everybody happy or haven't you heard!

The rich can always keep their large cars for luxury purposes or whatever, who knows, and the average man can keep his small car for pocketbook purposes. What's the difference? As long as everybody is satisfied. America will see to that. Although all countries do not produce cars, virtually every country contributes some part of make-up of the final product being sold.

So let's hear it for our automobile industry, red carpet and all!

Have a nice day and a better tomorrow!

And the Airlines are still #1 because you won't find a bat or bird with more speed and comforts.

III

Words

Words—let's count—is a 5-letter word. What then do the letters mean? Words are a means of communication and are dominant in all forms of socializations. The words we speak can express our thoughts to the fullest, carrying a point with little effort.

Just as people and situations help you adjust to a surrounding, so, too, do words which definitely get you established in any area of civilization. Words are relevant to the majority of earth's inhabitants. What new word or philosophy will you think of today, to help you deal with today's blocks? What word will you use today to help you get through the night? What clever word will you find to help you deal with yourself? Now try taking words away from communication and you will find a lost world with no destination!

Speaking of words, when you get some of them together they can form some very bizarre structures and interpretations. For example, the positions words fall in can have a lot to do with the message to be conveyed; many businessmen, politicians, teachers, lawyers, students and doctors use certain everyday words constantly to form ideas and patterns. The comedian especially is adept in this area, because he is constantly using funny words to entertain and arouse his audience. Words are a part of his occupation, so he passes them on for his listening audience to hear, so they may profit from this ancient but very strange art.

But you see, people constantly use all forms of words to get their point over. I used to know of this sergeant from Siberia who rode into this Army camp for a few months of assignment duty. After being there a while he started complaining about the area being so desolate, so empty, no women—which made him very horny. So he asked the other men what they did for their sex life since there were no women around, and the men pointed straight ahead and said "the camel over there!" Well the sergeant being a Casanova and strictly a lady's man, looked at the men and said, "Oh, no fellows, not me!"

So a few weeks began to pass, then months and this sergeant decided he couldn't take it anymore, so he went over to the camel, dropped his pants, and began working himself to death until he wore himself plain out. Now all this time the sergeant wasn't aware of the audience he had behind him and as he turned around tired as a dog, he smiled and said, "Is this the way you do it men?" And they said, "Why, no sir, sergeant, we just ride it into town, sir!"

So you see, words and the way you hear them and receive them can mean all the difference in the world in communications. People many times misinterpret words, taking a different meaning than the one implied and miss the boat completely. There was a lack of communication from the beginning. People can't understand something clearly if they don't first hear it clearly. I had a foreign friend of mine tell me once she thought her typewriter was pregnant because it missed a period. All people's levels of perception are not the same. Some need more attention than others. Of course you probably already know that.

Have you ever met anyone in your life who tells a lie everytime he opens up his mouth? Just yapping and boasting away and lying himself crazy? Ask him after payday does he have the money he owes you. "No, but I'll gladly pay you on my next. All the extra money I had went out to creditors and I hardly got two cents left now to carry me through my next payday." But this guy will swear to you that he's no liar and you better not let him hear you call him one either cause he will dispute you to his end. No doubt such a person is very familiar to you all.

You may find some of your greatest leaders are liars. That shouldn't shock too many of you out there, it being such common knowledge. Their lines come at you as swift and smooth as a butterfly's graceful landing, many times holding these powerful key leaders in their positions and purposely triggering off a mental chain reaction among their supporters.

There will never be a day in your life that you won't run into a lie in some form or fashion. You might find it in your home surrounding, your job, from siblings or anywhere you may be outside the home. Of course, you may be among the lucky ones who may not get stung as often as your friends. Still, these terrible lies never seem to have an ending, because when one lie is finished running its course, here comes another one usually not far behind; often its objective is to cover up or support the first one.

Lies and people are best described in one word—gullible. The most level-headed people sometimes find difficulty in dealing with the truth. To some, a lie is easier to believe than the truth, most probably because of the many flaws and snags in the structure of these misfits.

There are so many types of liars. First we have the liar who can be found in your social surroundings with one of the most ragged, unorganized and sloppiest presentations of a lie you ever heard. We will call him the "blundering liar," who for the life of himself cannot tell a lie straight. He will not look you in the eyes when he talks to you because he cannot. His speech is choppy and any fool could tell this man isn't right. To be downright blunt, his approach is very messy.

Our second type we'll call the "occasional liar" who can be found to some degree in us all. This kind lies sometimes to get himself out of a tight situation he may find himself involved in, for example, money to creditors. A good lie may hold off the vultures for awhile, at least. Most times this in-between liar would rather not lie but finds himself occasionally in difficulty. Many of us fall here.

Now this last type of liar stands ten feet tall in a world all alone and can be found extremely difficult to deal with if you try. Let's call him the "habitual liar." He will look you dead in the eyes and lie without a hint of guilt. As a matter of fact this type of liar is so consistent with his lies that he begins to believe them himself. His lines begin to sound true to him. If you can recall reading earlier about the professional con man, you can easily tie in the habitual liar, since the two relate so strongly. Lying comes easily to them because they lie like they gamble—recklessly!

Speaking of lies, I remember a fairytale I ran across once in grammar school. This book astonished me so much that still today the story remains very clear in the back of my head—and talking about lies, my friend, this book had trails of them running concurrently. Not taking anything away from its message though, the book was extremely exciting, well put together and, some claim, educational. Well, I go along with that. It was in our library under the "Mature Reading Section."

It involved a story about a little girl who went to sea . . . solo. She had the strength to perform an impossible task that no man living or dead today has ever accomplished. Are you ready for this? This girl swam across the ocean. Now don't ask me which one because the book didn't say, but you better believe whichever ocean she did choose, I bet she couldn't drink it all. This girl met a very unusual friend, during her journey, who happened to be a shark. Hold back now, just hold it down while I explain. I know and you know that in this day and time, sharks are deadly enemies. With all the research circulating concerning this dilemma, that should also be common knowledge.

Anyway, this shark and kid became the best of friends. I found it particularly funny the way they met. This girl by now was beginning to get tired treading all that water, as who wouldn't. So about the time she was completely about exhausted and going down for the last time, along comes this shark from nowhere and told her, "Hold on to my fins, baby, I'll guide you through."

Well, at this point I figured he had his stomach in mind, but I was wrong.

So all this time children readers have probably been thinking how they would really like to meet a shark that friendly. I had a kid tell me once, "Who could ever afford to go around the world any cheaper than that. This way, I can save all my money from my piggy bank and use it for the good times across the waters."

Finally this girl gets across this gigantic ocean, sick and tired as a dog. As a token of his appreciation to her, his guest through the whole ordeal, the shark takes her out to dinner.

Well, swell, I guess. Medium, rare or well done. Anyway after they left the restaurant, the shark made his exit and went back to his old familiar grounds, the water. He wished her much happiness and luck, and they waved good-bye until neither could see the other. As she walked on and on, she ran into some mice who had vocal chords, so they used them to talk. I told you this book was a solid trip and even the little girl decided this was too much for her to even try to handle, so she cut out. On her way out she ran into a cat who was having similar problems. He had just run into a pack of these talking mice so he, too, was on his way out. So the two decided to book out together. They walked and walked for days along the shores and finally ran into a ship of sailors who offered them both free rides back across the waters. They took this offer gladly.

The essence of this story goes like this: Wherever you find words, you will find some creation. Everybody tells lies, but the tricky part comes at the beginning and the end—when to lie and how often, if at all. Deal with it! Always be alert, open-minded and direct in your speech. This will provide you with smooth, cool sailing the rest of your way around.

Of course now I'm no angel myself when it comes to telling tales once in awhile. Everybody's got it in their blood to some degree, but some of us take it to an extreme, lying just for the hell of it. My rear end still reminds me of the whipping my mother and father and sometimes grandmother would give to me and my twin sister for lying during my childhood days. Shucks, my sister and I would get so many whippings that we knew one was coming each day when we arrived home from grammar school, because the teacher always had her report handy. We were seldom surprised because this was something we regrettably expected. Ever since then, I make it a practice never to tell a lie. Well, O.K., maybe a fib or two might slip out occasionally.

But whatever your game remember, lies eventually do come to surface. They may be extremely slow about surfacing, but once they do float to the top, watch out! Things can become too hot to handle, forcing you to jump around for days.

So the next time you lie, prepare yourself for a follow-up, which is, in turn, bound to need an encore, because this is what creates gossip, one of the most widely used forms of personal slights practiced today. The public can read about gossip in the newspapers, see it on television and commonly run into it at their job, where the daily news always concerns the executives, secretaries, and workers. Here is where gossip is commonly referred to as firsthand information because of its sources.

Gossip has existed since Genesis, so you may wonder what the world might be like without it. Gossip could be rated as indispensable to the "let's tear that so-and-so apart" group. Get-together socials also prove to be the only time for friends—watch that word—to get together and talk about good times, or can be just a plain dumb excuse to gossip along with the rest of the group, without being tagged as the instigator of the story.

When was the last time you sat down and got in on a little gossip? Was it interesting and informative? I don't know many people who don't enjoy listening to gossip. Most people, however, would rather not contribute any significant news on the pigeons being put up for discussion, simply because, when the word usually gets back around, the instigator turns out to be the person who made the least contribution to the conversation. Those of you who have been the scapegoat know how frustrating, irritating and hot this whirlpool can be, and many times can cause you to lose a dear friend because of misunderstanding. A person is innocent until proven guilty by the court of law, which is why the legal system here in America works a full twenty-four-hour schedule plus overtime. After the news media finishes, the public around the world have already made their conclusions and prematurely convicted and decided the fate of the pigeon, whoever he may be.

People in general usually believe what the news media announces first about an issue or individual to be enough proof it is true and most times it is. Those statements sometimes are the determining factor in what will make or break an individual, group or institution. The outcome can be devastatingly shocking and eminently surprising, which many of you already know from your own experience.

There is no adventure greater than gossip and no mystery greater than being its subject. It's something that wears on you till death do you part. There isn't one of you out there that can't remember your first dealings with gossip, especially if you were "the discussion."

There are also many tangibles involved here, relating to the basic structure of gossip and even how to avoid gossip. For example, take the five senses you are born with. Unfortunately for some, they may be minus a sense or two, either through birth defect or some accident during the later years. Still, those people are gifted in some other way to make up for their loss just like every other man and woman. Now these five senses, in some direct and indirect way, will set the tempo as to how effective your life might be. Let's start with sight. Now the average human who only has one eye can see well enough to observe the who's, what's, when's, where's and how's of living. But to see something without complete vision can be spiritually joyful. Then there are those people who have complete or partial vision and in gossip this can be quite advantageous, because you can see the "liar."

Hearing is also a useful tool because even if you can't see the instigator, you can hear this menace go off constantly satisfying his damn ego. Let the fool continue, it's a part of his life. He finds great pleasure in tearing somebody else down and putting himself up. He thrives on gossip and in order for him to be a part of the hip set, he's got to know all the dirt on everybody else first.

Now the next three senses can exist or not exist in the environment of gossiping since seeing and hearing are the most widely used instruments when being exposed to gossip. But let's hit on the other three anyway, starting with taste. Now I don't know how most people are when it comes to good food, but I love to taste mine. It is relatively safe to say there is no other substitute for taste—either you can taste your foods or you can't. Of course, if you like the smell of good cooking or sensuous fragrances then you are using your smelling sense constantly. Everybody loves the smell of something, be it plain musk or exotic scents.

Take your hands, the palm of your hands and rub them over your favorite thing. Yeah, if it's a person, touch that too. Don't you like the way it feels! Is it suitable to your touch system? Does it move you emotionally to feel your husband, your wife, your friend, your lover? If you're like most people, it feels great, otherwise you wouldn't be there wasting your time or theirs.

Everyone has a past but not a future. Your friends, your enemies, where does life begin? ESP is what some call a sixth sense and very few people are gifted with this trait. You may know the reason and destination of an individual or groups before the people themselves know. In most cases you know, before the rest of the world knows, what's about to happen and the effects are sometimes damaging because you know too much, too soon. Gossiping is like that too, only difference it's the complete opposite—knowing too much too fast amounting to not knowing anything!

Words are described as living things.
So what, then, do these letters mean?
To some it is a rebirth for a mind that is lost and in need.
These words that we speak can say so much in a verbal sense.
Express themselves beyond all odds, then come out in the form of communication.

There are words that are strong.
There are words that are weak.
There are words that are cold, shrewd and obnoxious.
There are words hot as fire.
There are words smooth and incandescent.
There is nowhere to hide from this mandatory language.
Now try and take words out of circulation and we would
become a lost world with no destination.

                —BEVERLY BETHEA GRIFFIN SHIPPY

IV

In Choosing
Partners

Everybody's got somebody somewhere, but are they happy? In many cases, the answer is no and the person inquires where this "somebody" can be found. So today, in our fast-paced world of modern technology, there are all types of methods available to help you meet your compatible partner.

Take for instance the computer Date-O-Matic. Now this computer diagnoses your case, through information you must supply, using different techniques which vary depending on the type of machine used. Anyway, this computer is supposedly going to come up with your perfect mate. Well, the truth of this matter is that no one is likely to come up with a mate perfect for you but you. No matter how much people claim you two were made for each other, the final decision lies between two people to decide who's compatible with whom—not a machine.

Of course, when it comes to building up your potential prospects based on quantity this computer can't miss; it makes an A here because it can screen your prospect list down to only those people with whom you share something in common and looking at the odds, that's pretty darn good. Most people look all their lives to just find people who share some common interests but continually run into incompatibility.

I had a friend to tell me once he was matched up with his sister. This computer transmitted the message that Margaret, the name I'll use here, was his perfect, compatible lover in all the ways he had described he wanted from of his mate; oddly enough, his sister looked for the same traits in her mate as well. So our computer matched the two as the most perfect of compatible mates. Well, when the two finally got together, they declined the offer and reentered their cards once again in the old faithful computer to try to select their perfect mates once again. My friend told me the machine exhibited a bit of humor, returning a message, after the two refed the computer: "I'm so sorry, but unfortunately we're not perfect either. Man designed us, too!"

You know that out there somewhere, there's a mate for each of us. I propose it's like a continuous turntable, revolving around and around until the eventual hook-up of your Romeo or Juliet. In most cases, however, in the love game as in many other games, you may only get one chance to grab it or lose it. Nothing more, nothing less. If you are fortunate enough to pin down your perfect mate the first time around, then you are indeed one of the luckiest people in the world. Divorce and separation pass you by. For the rest of those looking, usually if you pass up one good potential, the right one may not come along again in ten years. But like all other things with life, your chance will come along again, another time. Be patient and wait. Yours is out there somewhere. Maybe not in your hometown but far out somewhere you would have never imagined it to be. Things alike attract each other—things unlike repel each other. Which force pulls you? When true love is present, people find some way to get together no matter how complex their situation may be.

In American society today, marriage is still the American way of life. We vow to honor and obey each other till death do us part. But somehow, someway, divorce may just slip right on in without any signal or warning at all, destroying every dream two people ever had once of building the utopian lifelong relationship together. Marriage then divorce. Why put the two of them together? Why not? You can't have one without the other.

American people today jump into marriage as quickly as they

jump out, which is the dominant factor in many break-ups. The different methods used in liquidating a marriage include annulment, which is the cheapest by far, depending on the state, length of time married and a few other legal complexities. If you want to know more about the legal aspects of divorce and the alternatives, get yourself a good law book that can be found in most libraries, or shop around for a reputable lawyer and take it from there. Those alternatives can direct you back to the right track again.

Separation, running second, can also be one of the less complicated routes to take, with each partner involved sketching out the agreements for a temporary trial separation.

Divorce is definitely the last alternative, which begins the hard detachment of material and emotional ties, piercing the pocketbook as well as the heart and sometimes leaving a permanent scar. The young children of such partners usually suffer the greatest pains in such a process because of the sudden two-party parental detachment. To put it plainly and simply—the children don't understand why. The scars left on them can sometimes be permanent as well.

Now since we know why people marry and divorce, let's see what factors enter into this institution. Could it be, love at first sight—those piercing eyes penetrating into you like a laser beam? Then you might want to consider the economy; with prices steadily rising, some couples figure four hands are better than two. Some might choose marriage for financial security assuming the love part coming eventually through time, patience and understanding. Then there are those couples who have gone together for years and now know they are made for each other.

Marriage is a contract whereby a man and a woman agree to enter into one union for better or worse till death do them part. Divorce is the complete opposite.

In the beginning there was man and woman. Nature saw to it the two would unite, forming one union, the family. Their most treasured gift from God was the ability to produce offspring.

The old wive's tale reads, a solid marriage is like grinding cement—the kind that doesn't break. A marriage, like anything else, takes time to grow into a better and more solid relationship for both partners involved. Marriage is serious business and the ultimate relationship when man and woman have found each other. Marriage is a man and woman loving each other and willing to share themselves with each other, giving their whole selves to each other and providing the comforts in life for each other.

Now, to get into the context of marriage and its elements and guidelines which work only for those who are most sincere at heart. Point number one: Have you ever sat down and tried to understand your husband's habits—your wife's habits? These habits at first may seem strange and absurd to you, deriving a strong resemblance from the cuckoo's nest, but they are still a part of your partner's personality. You must try to accept them. If this annoyance is getting beyond control, a simple or complex agreement will have to be devised. Whichever works out better for you, then sit down and discuss it. Most habits can just as easily be dismissed as they are acquired. Habits are made to be broken and if this habit is beginning to destroy both of you—kill it first. Destroy it. Now some habits may be physical and need a doctor's prescription to cure. But in this case, both of you could use the same procedure, first discussing the possible alternatives between yourselves, then heading directly to your friendly family physician's office. You'd be surprised at some of the small things that break up marriages.

Maybe your husband snores so loud when he sleeps that even the chickens are beginning to complain. Maybe your wife sleeps restlessly, unconsciously belting you around at night in her sleep. Both of these are physical problems and could be very difficult to correct. A solution: For that noisy husband of yours, encourage him to sleep on his stomach more often, instead of his back. People who snore are usually very restless before retiring anyway, so the subconscious mind initiates within the body a rejection system to throw off all that extra tension which the body must release, in snoring. By the way, extremely loud snoring is a tremendous strain on the heart and in the long run could cause some form of heart damage. One method to relieve snoring is to rub him down good once a night, at first, until his condition appears to be getting less, then only give him a good rubdown two or three times a week. Massage his whole body vigorously and firmly until his muscles relax. Use a couple of hot towels and spread them over his entire body, making sure he is wrapped completely for about ten minutes, then remove the towels and send him off to bed. He'll sleep like a baby. Men like to be cuddled and cared for like babies sometimes. They love it. Repeat this process as often as necessary, until it is obvious he is improving.

As for the wife's wild sleeping habits, she should ask her husband to buy a bigger bed, so that her sleeping annoyances don't try his nerves any longer. If you have a regular size bed maybe the king size bed would be the better choice by far for all. Also the mattress could have a lot to do with sleeping habits. Shop around for a different type of mattress that feels better than the old one. A bad mattress as well as small beds can make a terrible sleeper out of anyone. Yes, understanding each other's habits can do a lot to strengthen a marriage and help both of you to contend with each other's habits or get rid of these habits. Break the habit and live.

Who handles the family finances? Now here is when you might run into the knock down, drag out fights, that end up downright disgusting. Why should two supposedly mature adults fight over who should handle the money? Compromise! If it is quite obvious Sam is too loose with the money let Mary handle it—plain and simple—or vice versa. This mismanagement of money can upset any household and turn it bottom side up. If both of you handle money pretty wisely, then that's solid and you should have no problems. Money comes hard but can get away faster than lightning and when a marriage partner lacks money management in even the simplest forms, then it is definitely time to appoint or designate the one who does exhibit some experience in building or working with the capital. If not, both of you could virtually end up in the poorhouse.

Who makes all the decisions? Now is the time for all wise men to come out and speak their piece. Effective decision-making, can key in even the highly underdeveloped individual and teach him to call the shots successfully and keep a consistent hand of spades. Decision-making in marriage takes the unanimous co-operation of both partners involved, only because the two of you are directly responsible for any decision the other one makes.

Decisions come out better for all involved if the rough draft is discussed first then laid out and taken apart around the kitchen table, the living room, the bedroom. Propose your decisions on a long term basis, first setting up your most important priorities, then your least. This is the way you find out what is most important to you. Once however you make that identification, you are now on the open road to a successful, fulfilling, everlasting love affair.

Do you encourage extra-marital affairs? Oh! Have you ever been driving your car and suddenly become lost? Well then, you know the feeling. You're numb! There's just emptiness inside that won't go away, so you just bear with it until your direction is clear again.

What's in it for you? An erotic thrill, revenge, escapism? Your environment is full of this kind of thing and that is why you chose to be married, because you were tired of this make-believe circle and you formed the family. There will always be tempta-tion and threats to any good thing, so there's no special exception for marriage. The key is where your mind is and what you repre-sent to yourself, your family.

Some of you may be wondering why divorce has not been discussed in extensive detail, showing what makes them work. Divorce *doesn't* work, that's why. Everyone wants to know what makes a divorce work. They don't. They come a dime a dozen and don't take much of nothing—yeah—that's the word—much of nothing.

Marriage—right on!

V

Time

What's "once upon a time?" Have you ever actually sat down for a moment and given deep thought to this mysterious force? Where did it come from and where does it go? Why can't we bring tomorrow back for another grand finale or put it in a bottle, placing the plug in for keeps?

Well in reality time is like this—you can't do anything with it. Time cannot be held back. It's here today, gone today, assumed to return continuously, non-stop tomorrows and perform its number over and over again. This we expect.

As you sit here reading and getting into your favorite sandwich, time is passing you by. Can you catch it? Just hold it down for one second. Go ahead and do it. Reach out quickly. Grab it! Now, while you'll making that big effort to catch that mysterious force, stop your clocks for a moment and turn back the hands of time. Even for this time-consuming thing, you can psyche yourself out psychologically for a while at least. Isn't it fun!

Scientifically speaking, you are the master of your own destiny. Life is based on time itself. So time goes on after life ends. Common sense is time-consuming since the longer one lives, the more common knowledge you should store up through the years. The instinct to survive is time-consuming. Time will be here, presumably, after you're dead and gone.

Many of us today are afraid to look deep within ourselves for help because we are afraid of what we might find. Then after we get over that shock the next step might be how to deal with what we find. People pattern their behavior then basically go through three stages in life called the feeling, the experience and the intellectual phases. But how can we successfully deal with either if we first don't know ourselves?

Let's find an object that gives off a complete image of ourselves. Let's find an image that is as complete and accurate as the time of day. An object that cannot lie, cheat or mislead because you will know the truth anyway. So as a result of your findings, you take this reflection of yourself for what it's worth. A dime, a nickel, a penny, a dollar. You're the boss, at least for right now anyway.

Let's find that object right now. Let's call it the mirror. The cheap glass you can buy in any five and dime store. The mirror gives off the most accurate complete picture of ourselves, highlighting every detail on the external surface. Yes, this glass fixture can be found somewhere in every home around the world reflecting numerous images of people with a single glance of the eye, showing your exact duplicate with no imitation flaws present.

So before you do anything destructive to yourself, find a mirror in your home that is temporarily blocked from any house traffic, then take a stand in front of it. Now look yourself over good from head to toe. If you want to get a closer look at that fantastic you, take off all those garments that hide your body beauty and just stare yourself down. What are you seeing? If you look at yourself long enough, you may find some interesting things about yourself you never observed before. No I am not referring to that red spot on your skin which is usually hidden. I'm referring to the naked body. I want you to take a good, long look at yourself, as mentioned earlier, from head to toe. Go ahead and laugh too if you see that body of yours a little funny. You are alone I presume so the laughter will only be heard by you. That's right folks, see yourself in living color and by the way what color are you? It doesn't matter anyway since mirrors don't discriminate.

The challenges of life are not just the daily routines you

experience but the complexities that involve those daily routines, the motivation, the drive.

If you don't believe you are the master of your own destiny, think awhile on this. Can you remember your last exciting, fun venture? Who manipulated you into participating? Your best friend, your lover, your marriage partner? One thing for sure is you were not forced to go anywhere. You went because you wanted to go. Your destiny chart indicated a need for you to go, so you went.

Who is responsible for that career you want to pursue or—for you lucky ones that may have reached your peak already—who's responsible for you staying there? Everything on earth is based on time. The sun rises every morning at a certain time. You retire every night at a certain time and for those of you who work nights, let's just reverse that sentence to the day, as your time for retirement. You see, I didn't forget about you either. Somebody has to work nights while the rest of the world sleeps. Everything you do is time-consuming. Common knowledge is time-consuming only because the longer you exist, the more common knowledge you accumulate. The instinct to survive is picked up from the environment and what determines all that . . . *TIME?*

I had an associate once tell me "your time is my time." Well, I had to tell my friend that's a lie. "You see, friend," I said, "time belongs to no one." We're all borrowing it for a while until we do our final number, then time will go on pacing with other people's lives until it winds itself completely down. We're all borrowing time for a while, until our final number is called, then time will go on for others to borrow and turn over and over and over revolving around like a wheel until time reaches its final number, its final turn, and stops!

Your destiny was determined the minute you entered this world. So don't be naive about this thing, because there is nothing you can do with it but accept it and work through it. Again sometime tonight before you turn in, go before your mirror-image again and take a stand, a sit or a squat. Maybe you might even want to lie down. But position yourself right there in front of that mirror until you are satisfied with what you see. What's that I hear? You want to put a paper bag over your head! Just let whatever you found there before you sink into your head then sleep on it. Dream about it. Tomorrow morning you could wake up a more total, complete, happier person. Then once you have found and accepted this new person, immediately outline ways to deal with this new person, your environment and your loved ones.

Who is responsible for your career? Who is responsible for your destiny? Who is responsible for your fate? What could you turn out to be if you were ever given the opportunity to reach your fullest potential? Where would you be now in your career?

Who is responsible for you? Time waits on no one. So now, what's your brilliant excuse?

VI

Astrology

Astrology is a science based upon the stars and their positions. It is a force just as unknown and mysterious as your destiny, a force that can warn you of your future in order for you to make any adjustments in meeting or avoiding your destiny. Astrology can do all this otherwise it would have died centuries ago. Now there are many of you out there who can't relate to astrology or would rather not associate with astrology. But like most creations, astrology has also been around since the beginning of time and once again is making a strong showing providing it is here to stay.

Many people are using astrology as daily guides to follow. Of course, this consistency can run you into big troubles or it might warn you of hazards in your day, making you more aware and careful throughout your day.

So I can assume it is safe to say astrology is a thing of the past, present and future. Those twelve so-different signs of the Zodiac are meaningful to many of us, while to others, they could care less whether or not the zodiac exists. They can take it or leave it. Why then does the zodiac exist? What was its purpose and how is it relating to the world's people? I, for one, occasionally read my horoscope and find myself falling sometimes right into that pattern for that particular day or month and sometimes the results can be spellbinding and surprising, because the forecast has you right down to a tee.

I had the opportunity to talk with a few folks concerning their feelings toward the Zodiac and share it with you now; the questions asked were in general terms that all ages could relate to.

Yes, astrology!! What do you think about it? Is it a thing of the past or is it, as the young folk say, what's happening!!! (The missing signs had no comments.)

AQUARIUS: "I read my horoscope everyday but don't believe a word of it. It's so general that it could fit anybody any day. You can take a Leo and put him in the chart with an Aquarius. It's all the same, very, very general. I don't believe a word of it but I read mine everyday!"

ARIES: "I believe them to the extent they apply to me. I don't govern my life by them. Par example, sometimes it may predict you are going to make a great fortune today but I'm not going out there and spend $100.00 trying to find it. Horoscopes are good for weak-minded people who need some daily advice to live by. You have to be the controller, you can't let it control you."

TAURUS: "As many people as there are in this particular sign, it would hit somebody everyday but not necessarily the same people everyday. Then too, it could hit the same people everyday. There are too many people born under the same sign for predictions to apply to the same person everyday. It's got to alternate."

CANCER: "I don't believe in it and I feel those people that do believe in it are weak. If it's not for Aries today, it's for Cancer tomorrow."

True, the zodiac signs are so different and mysterious in their own ways, it might be a total disaster to take them away from the history books. If we decided to put all these unique but so-different signs into twelve nutshells, then we could identify each of them this way: begin with the Ram, the sign of birth, Alpha, the beginning, and end with the Fish, the sign of death, or Omega. If you possess some humor within your soul, let's go into something real deep here—let's call it your zodiac personality. NOTE:

The following has no direct bearing on your future; it only gives you insight on what you are like.

ARIES (*Ram*): March 20-April 19. You hold most people in contempt when met on a one to one basis because you are the pioneer type. You become very scornful when given advice, and are extremely impatient and quick-tempered. A word most appropriate for you Ram, a jerk.

TAURUS (*Bull*): April 20-May 20. If nothing else, Taurus, you are very persistent and practical, period. Your determination can be said to be downright dogged in effort, which makes you not mind working like hell for any of your goals. Most people find you stubborn, a bit bull-headed or both. You are the geniuses of material wealth and nothing other than goddam COMMUNISTS. That is meant to be a harmless figure of speech.

GEMINI (*Twins*): May 21-June 20. Your mind is very swift as compared to the other eleven houses which makes you quick on your feet and an intelligent thinker. People may find you to be a little strange because you are bisexual. You tend to run people away from you fast because you expect too much too soon for so little. To put it bluntly, you are cheap. Geminis are famous for thriving on their infected egos.

CANCER (*Crab*): June 21-July 22. You are very understanding, which makes you sympathetic to other people's problems. They may even take you for a sucker every once in a while because of your consistency in always putting things off. That is one of the reasons you will always be on welfare and not worth two damn cents.

LEO (*Lion*): July 23-Aug. 22. The Lion is considered to be the born leader of the Zodiac so don't worry when other people find you to be too pushy. Most lions are perfectionists, while being bullies, so that's the reason they refuse to accept criticism and appear to be vain constantly. Their sense of arrogance is downright disgusting. No wonder most of you are the King of Jackasses.

VIRGO (*the Virgin*): Aug. 23-Sept. 22. Born gifted with the trait of logical thinking and attention to fine detail which is the reason you hate disorder. Although your constant nitpicking is sickening among friends, nevertheless it is a part of your personality; you are nothing if not cold and unemotional, often falling asleep while making love.

LIBRA (*Scales*): Sept. 23-Oct. 22. Libra, being the artistic type you are you will have a difficult time in dealing with reality. If you happen to be a man, you are likely to be very creative and dealing with career changes, money and promotional climbs will prove excellent for you. Most Libra women are pure nymphomaniacs. Many Libras are destined to die from an overactive sex life leading to heart attacks.

SCORPIO (*Scorpion*): Oct. 23-Nov. 21. You are the shrewdest of persons when dealing in business as well as love affairs and cannot be trusted as far as the eyes can see. You will most likely achieve the pinnacle of success with little difficulty, because of your icy attitude in the lack of logical ethics. That is the reason most of you are carefully murdered.

SAGITTARIUS (*the Archer*): Nov. 22-Dec. 21. Sagittarians are enthusiastic and optimistic people in all endeavors which drives them recklessly into relying on pure luck since they themselves lack talent. You may find the great majority of these archers are alcoholics or dope addicts. People laugh at you so often because you are always available for the bed.

CAPRICORN (*the Goat*): Dec. 22-Jan. 19. Since you are so conservative Capricorn, you are optimistic about taking risks. Why? Because you don't do much of anything and are lazy. There have been few Capricorns of great importance, that is why you, of all signs, should avoid standing out in the open for long periods of time. You tend to attract pigeons.

AQUARIUS (*the Water Bearer*): Jan. 20-Feb. 18. Your mind is very inventive, Aquarius, which inclines you to be progressive. You lie a great deal. Reversing that behavior, your mistakes are constantly repeated because of your impracticality and carelessness. Many people think you are downright stupid.

Pisces (*the Fish*): Feb. 19-Mar. 20. Pisces, you have an overactive imagination which imposes on you the constant paranoia of thinking you are being followed by the CIA or FBI. Since you have minor influence over your associates some people resent you when you start flaunting your power. The sex life of these creatures is always full and exciting.

This is the end of your horoscope personality. Please note that the stars and the moon do not have a direct bearing on your destiny but only expand your destiny to make certain events obtainable to you if you happen to take advantage of its influence. IT MUST NOT RULE YOUR LIFE.

VII

Ethnic Background

People of all cultures pattern their behavior on the mores of the group. As civilized human beings, for instance, we all know it is highly unethical to walk around the streets naked. We just don't do that here in America. We wear clothes when we go outside the home or go to jail.

Generally people go through three stages during their lives, called the feeling, experience, and intellectual phases. People love to feel both their inner and outside emotions connected with their soul. People constantly go through some phases of stress in everyday life. The longer one lives, the more experiences he has to call upon. The longer one lives, the more he uses his intellectual side and wits to challenge ideas, laws and experiments.

Throughout your patterns of living you will use the coping behaviors generally associated with laughing, regressing and manipulating. Over 65 percent of our messages are nonverbal because we have found a universal language available every nationality knows of and can decipher. It's called nonverbal expressions. Facial expressions, eye movements and body movements—everybody can relate to that. Can't we! For example, if you don't like a particular food you accidentally run across, the expression on your face will automatically show how displeased you are. Did you know it takes more muscles to frown than it does to laugh? People's reactions always show when they like or dislike something or someone, most times without having to say a word to anyone. Look at their faces!

You hang out with nice people you get nice friends. Corrupt people bring you corrupt friends. Birds of a feather always flock together. Most traits picked up in life are acquired somewhere along the way and those traits not acquired are inherited. Like growth, anything acquired also takes time to develop through time, through socializations, through the environment.

Race education is picked up here more so than in any other system because of our multiracial society. Now if you will notice, we are entering the area of likes and dislikes, which can range from one extreme to the other, depending greatly on the individual. Some people like to spread theirs around, while others would rather remain passive. Which one are you?

What causes people to like or dislike something. Why would you prefer to live on the East Coast instead of the West Coast. What makes you like one band name of coffee better than others? Do we all acquire our likes and inherit our dislikes or could it be the other way around or could it be neither?

Let's experiment and see. Let's experiment with a topic that's just as familiar to the world as the knowledge of income tax. Let's call it the dealings between races—Caucasians and Blacks.

All races of the world have extensive historical backgrounds which nurtured what we are today. As a matter of fact these races have been around since cave man days.

Blacks and Caucasians have been here on earth for centuries. Some still find difficulty accepting and adjusting to what the others represent today. Being from different racial backgrounds and different cultural traditions, naturally indoctrinates each race to practice their own individuality and the races can't seem to understand why other races behave as they do. Well, for one thing, both races go back many, many centuries. It is impossible to put one hand on their differences. It is impossible to change the already written history of these two distinctively different cultures.

Asians, Hispanics, Blacks, Caucasians, Orientals—each has been on this planet for centuries, so you see no one race owns America. Now Venus or Pluto I'm not too sure about, but earth for all we know, belongs to all men. Look at your churches. The above races break even as far as discrimination goes. All of those groups know what discrimination feels like and what's happening there but apart from so many barriers, each race managed to survive and contribute to the birth of America. Every race has contributed here even if it was small. But who can say what is small or large for that matter. Maybe God can.

The old saying that all men are created equal is true. "God put us here on the intended terms no man is greater or better than the other, but every man given a gift of determination and common knowledge to use or repress it as a tool to venture out into any phase he wants and challenges."

So now America, since God put so many different races and their cultures here on earth together, why are we still fighting one another? Accept each race as they are and be thankful you are a living contributor to our rich, beautiful land called America. After all it was created for every man and woman to live in and believe me there's land here on earth for every man, woman and child to own a piece of and still have plenty left over. So let's get off of all those old fashion attitudes. Face reality and accept all races of the world. They would never have been put here if not to contribute to the founding of a great nation, America.

Every human race is as different as night and day. Not solely because of skin pigmentation but because of society's attitudes and cultural ancestry. There is nowhere in the world where you can go today and not run into one race or the other, in some situation, even if your stay is only temporary. Of course, you might run into the following type of person. Let's check out the man or woman who can just curl your skin—the bigot. This person, who can be found any and everywhere, uses as his weapon his mind to fight against any force that opposes his absurd behavior. Statistically speaking everyone of us are bigots to varying degrees, because we all possess some form of prejudice.

The bigot usually creates all kinds of confusion. He creates animosity among friends, associates and partners. His behavior is so perverted and obstinate that a jackass donkey would catch hell running against him. They would probably kick each other's rear end so much that they would eventually have to find some peaceful way of compromising or turn to wearing diapers.

Usually after this bigot makes himself perfectly clear, he then begins creating inferiority complexes among friends. These people begin letting their subconscious mind take over, resulting in this individual failing. This is a sign of weakness. Never let your inner strength succumb to your weaker side. You know what happens then maybe better than I—you lose.

One thing for sure—no race is going extinct which means each representative race will definitely be here until eternity. So let's hear it, America, for all races of the world. Take people for what they are and leave the color thing alone.

VIII

Rejecting Behavior Cop-Outs

Now some of you have gone through this book and not understood anymore than before you started. Reading and reading on, then not remembering one damn thing you read afterwards is because of your brought-on despondency, which was with you before you began reading.

That's all right—that's fine. Remember what I said earlier? Oh, I forgot. You can't remember anything. Well, I don't mind repeating it again. Here goes. I began by saying not to worry too much about this problem because all kinds of people make up this world so, just like you, there are a million more of you out there somewhere that feel the same way. Some of you get so uptight sometimes over mediocre things that you are forced to make a bad decision and reject the plugs that come and go throughout your lives, so the final alternative is suicide.

You've decided to throw in the disc and call it quits. The coward takes that route too, because just like you, he too has finally lost all his will power to live further and work at growing out of the problems that have him temporarily all balled up into knots. It takes just as much brain power to kill oneself as it does to mentally figure out how to wriggle out of that mess you've gotten yourself into. All men run into hardships at some point in their lives and with will power and the help of God they can usually wiggle back out. But it takes perseverance.

So for heaven's sake don't cause others close to you to suffer, too, from your weakness. You may have finally gotten your chance to exit from your confused land but will you really find paradise in that other land. Is that land so different from ours that it is persuading you to enter it slightly ahead of your time.

Wait a minute, won't you. Just take your time now. Take it easy. Don't be in such a hurry to journey into that land we call the unknown. Before you make your final decision to leave us here, wait a while and go away from all your problems with a close friend, marriage partner, relative or anyone you feel very close to and who you feel will honestly understand your desperate need for help. A WORD OF WARNING: Do take someone with you. Rule number one—do not go it alone because it won't work. This is one of those times you desperately need someone to work with you and help you to pull yourself back together again, to help you pull yourself back into reality. If you have to take a leave of absence from work for a while, leave it temporarily and stay away as long as it will take you to get yourself back together again. A life is a terrible thing to waste and nothing in this world can ever take its place. If you are working with a fairly reputable company large or small, they will understand your problem. People get sick or whatever and take a leave of absence for many reasons worse than yours everyday, then return when things become better. Here's a suggestion you might want to remember that will work for you. There is always someone else out there worse off than you. Remember that always.

You know for a land so rich and beautiful, so full of all the natural resources anyone could possibly need for a full and rich rewarding life, there is nothing in the world as precious and dear as the life of a human being. For God saith "Whosoever believeth in Me will not perish but have everlasting life." He gave up his only begotten son, Jesus Christ, who shed his own blood so that all men would live forever and you mean to sit here today feeling so sorry for yourself that you've decided to give up everything including your life! Rule number two. Pack up and leave everything behind you. Begin immediately referring to that scene as your last. Take a trip to a far away place, which could end up in a long stay or short stay, depending solely on you. But do remember rule number one. Don't go alone. Now you may have tremendous obligations back home that depend desperately on your financial support, but for those of you who have tried everything already, including a psychiatrist, and your life still isn't working out for you then the only thing left to do is to pack up and leave. Those obligations will have to be delayed until the provider has made a recovery. Go to a remote place where there aren't many people around to distract you or influence you. You and the closest person to you will be enough company for each other to let it all hang out. Let everything go! You must cry yourself out until there isn't a tear left. Open yourself up to your friend—yourself. Tell yourself why you have to live over and over again. Tell yourself you will conquer this problem and live to help others like yourself who feel your way. Tell yourself there is nothing better than life itself and that is where everything is at!

Most people who turn to killing themselves don't have enough common sense left to reason intelligently anymore so they close up communication and become despondent. Then fate races toward them top speed, pinning its victim tight in all his confusion and causing the act of his own hand to take away *LIFE*.

So take that get-away trip away somewhere as your last alternative. This goes for those people who also suffer from a mental breakdown. It's all the same. One thing can lead to another. Do it, because it *WILL* work for you. If you can afford a head doctor you can surely afford a vacation that will make all the difference in your life that your psychiatrist couldn't. Now I'm not saying to put down your psychiatrist. You won't find a more efficient and thorough association of professionals anywhere else in the world. But, when therapy doesn't work, go to the next best thing. You have everything to gain. You get short-changed enough by just living day to day in some way or another. Don't cheat yourself. When your time comes God will call you.

If you take a second just to think of all the sick people in the medical centers around the world who are constantly fighting for their life against some dreadful disease you will see they have been fighting, praying and hoping to pull through. They're fighting for their lives everyday to just survive through their illness and be able to live on. You have to realize that these people are physically sick, not mentally sick, which takes more physical as well as mental strength to fight off their disease than many of you physically and mentally well individuals can imagine. But somehow, some way, they may pull through and get well again because they have the desire to live. Temporary setbacks don't defeat them. They only defeat you, because you are weak. Behind us lies our beginning—birth. Ahead of us lies the inevitable—death. Not many people can easily accept or understand this final phase. Of course, acceptance depends on the experience one has gained throughout his life.

We did not ask for life, but somehow we're here living and breathing and functioning everyday until our time runs out. Life is short. All of us have temporary or even a few permanent hang-ups but we don't all handle them the same way. Do we all defeat our purpose for being given the gift of life. Do we all fall easily to defeat. It takes strong hands to pull the final plug on oneself, but that same energy used in the reverse can redevelop a strong mind and hand to withstand that temptation which will lead to nowhere but up dead-ends creek.

I, for one, could imagine that ground gets cold as hell in the winter. You can lead a cow to green pastures, but if his mind ain't right, he won't know what to do. Some people are like that too. When people can't function at all, we can expect suicide. Depression is a part of life and fits into the cycle of living, much like a roller coaster is shifting constantly.

GOD LOVES YOU SO MUCH!

IX

Motivational Instruments

It is not the style of clothes one wears.
It is not the number of friends one has.
These mean nothing when dealing with success.
The meaning of success is simply service.
That is the only factor that measures success.
—BEVERLY BETHEA GRIFFIN SHIPPY

Tomorrow begins the rest of your life.

Get up right now and stop whatever you're doing and pick up your newspaper. Glance over the front page at the headlines. If you would take notice, some of the headlines will attract your attention right away while others mean nothing. What interests you the most? Does it consist of mainly all violence, or does the paper pull your interest in all directions.

Generally if our newspapers want to sell it's what's put up front from the very beginning that sells—not always the newspaper in general but the "headlines." These are the high points. This is what sells. Of course, there are always a few exceptions to the rule involving those newspapers that are already prestigious and top-rated here in America, the ones that can still get away with junk every now and then. They also know not to repeat this pattern too often, knowing that enough is enough and when to stop this nonsense.

Just the other day while skimming through the classified ad section, it was very interesting to observe how the wording of these ads can be so misleading, one-sided and often filled with incorrect (*sic*) spelling.

For example some companies run the ad in the paper knowing that they have already chosen their prospective employee but by law, they must advertise it publicly first. So in order to avoid suit, these companies must go through this long ordeal of running their ads in the big issue generally published on Sunday. If people never buy a newspaper any other day, which there are few, they will buy it on Sunday. Now as Monday rolls around, you are now prepared to give this ad some play. In your pursuit, you call this company before noon to set up an appointment for an interview. But you might hear "I'm sorry, but this position has already been filled," or even, "I'm so sorry, but we are no longer taking applications because we have reached our limit."

The frequency of all these disappointments begin to cluster one's nerves, bringing about frustration and hostility toward classified ads. You're not satisfied with looking on your own because you're continually getting negative results. So a dear friend of yours may hip you to the employment agency route, letting them find the right job for you. Now some of these agencies are fee-paid but many are not. You may get stuck with the agency which asks for a fee according to your job placement. You also may know that some of these employment agencies are the biggest ripoffs going around town but you really gotta get that job—you may even be desperate by now, so as the final result, you throw yourself on the mercy of your job counselor, who must find that ideal job for you. Besides, when *you're rewarded, he's rewarded.* By draw now, that's fair play! Now if you would take note: all agencies or businesses are ripoffs. They say they strive to serve purposes for the good of mankind. Only the one-legged ones in operation today may be influential in convincing the public they are all bad. Businesses are rich because they serve you, the public.

Now as I was saying, these ads really get obnoxious to a point. Some of the glamor school ads that often read, "Become a professional model or just look like one." Now the average girl who's looking for prestige, or just from curiosity, might jump at this opportunity to experience, for awhile at least, the very glamorous life that goes along with being the professional model. But what many fail to know and realize is that after completion of their school training, which could end in as little as three months or last up to two or more years, there are no guaranteed positions open to these young women or men, as they expected. Some will make prize landings, others will not find jobs, or maybe never at all. So there you have it, all that training and nowhere to use it, because nobody will give you that chance you need. As a result, you're out there hustling for your life, trying to get that one break. Let someone see me. And they will, providing you stay out there long enough and have the patience and perseverance to wait it out.

Now while your struggle is still going strong, along comes the miracle man who can tie all ragged ends together, no matter how choppy they may appear. Your miracle man may identify himself as an agent. Not taking anything away from his thing, many times this agent can give you an excellent deal while your feet are still damp, because this is the time both of you need each other the most. Solid Cold Cash. But as a rule, forewarned is forearmed; you must first ride for awhile on the merry-go-around, revolving around and around like a twister in disguise until you get off plain dizzy and confused, causing you to change agents frequently as the weeks fly by. This even holds true for the veteran in the job-hunting business, who also rides this merry-go-round many times, not knowing what might happen next. But with your strong desire, you stick with that ride until your day comes along. The keen vulture never sleeps, only naps. Now, when your luck does hit, *CAN YOU HANDLE IT?*

Let's face it. If you want your career badly enough, you will have to work on merit and the training which you had awhile back. On top of that you're going to be suffering a minor or major psychological brain beating with one hell of a headache, which tends to cling to the climber like a leech. Then, after you reach your goal, the headaches become a part of the price connected with your title and this, too, comes along with success. That goes for any occupation, not just the beat of the entertainment business. Only the strong will survive! This means you must always have positive attitudes—positive pursuit!

You know some people have a natural talent for the theatre world whereas the other 60 percent do not. All people are not born to be actors and actresses. Since it takes all types of people to make up the theatre world, that is exactly what the American entertainment world is composed of—all types of people. Well, that's only natural, wouldn't you think? Our society is full of all kinds of people so why not have that same representation in the theatre.

Look around at your leading box-office thespians and you won't find any two of them alike. They're each as different as night and day both in character and color. As you may already know, they have them in all colors, too. To name a few here we may occasionally run into brown, yellow, white, mulatto, black, you name it and you will run across it. Although the theatrical arts will be a very glamorous and rich profession for the highly paid group, the benefits are unpredictable. All potential models and thespians have one thing they can truthfully say they share in common and that is the element of perfect timing, a lot of good luck and plenty of hard work. The reward can be a long overdue, short rest for your efforts and big advancement in that career of yours. Sounds good.

Of course we all can help ourselves a lot more if we would use more of our acquired instinct called motivation. Many of us miss out on that once-in-a-life time opportunity, because we lack the motivation, the drive to go after our wants, our needs. We don't quite understand how to connect these two variables together, so we continue to remain in the backfield, hoping and praying for fresh luck. You must get out there and make luck work for you.

There are numerous types of motivational instruments available today that people are using to push themselves forward. Most people need a crutch to keep them going, to help support their drive. There's nothing wrong with this, as long as this crutch isn't hazardous to your health. This crutch has to have a name, so we'll call it the "positive initiator," which varies extensively depending on the individual using the instrument.

For example, if you have been working towards a project for quite some time and truthfully feel within yourself that you have made great progress then do yourself a favor. Give yourself a reward. Just as the famous French scientist Pavlov rewarded his dogs with food reinforcement every time they progressed, try that same technique on yourself. Feed yourself a banana—no, entertain a few guests over at your place; take your husband, wife or children out for the weekend. Do something. Reward yourself for that accomplishment. Dogs and human beings are no different when it comes to rewards. Both are very malleable and with reinforcement will go forward not backward. Of course now by rule, dogs will need more reinforcement, more frequently than humans only because their attention span is much shorter. The human being, however, is far more intelligent than the animal when it comes to reinforcement rewards, simply because the human being possess intellectual stamina able to wait out problems and letdowns analytically. So, reinforcement is a positive initiator only because those who choose to use this instrument have found out it works. As a result people are very receptive to this reinforcement.

Another example of a positive initiator might be a promotion on your job, which results in higher pay. Now this is definitely positive reinforcement. Another example of an instrument might be a citation for your excellent services throughout your years of dedication on the job. You'll be compelled to continue doing better, because others appreciate your services.

So whatever your crutch might be, continue using it only if it's making things work out for you. Whether it's your career life or your love life, it's your life and you don't have to get permanently stuck with anything you don't want. A word for you— get out early, for heaven's sake, and pursue your interest. Here's all you have to do, in the following order only:

1. Organize your strategy.
2. Work on your thoughts and how you want to deliver them.
3. Pursue.

On speaking earlier concerning computers, some folks seem to think there're some people out there that never need help. But if you are able to sleep, eat and work, you already know this is not true. Everybody needs help once in awhile.

For example, with all the road maps in the world available to anyone, when you become lost in a foreign city not familiar to you, you may ask someone for directions. That's help.

Imagine yourself just beginning to top off this new business you've had eyes on for quite some while. You know you'll be sitting tight as far as money is concerned. But everybody, it doesn't matter who you are, can always use a little bit more. So being a business cleave, as you are, you practice quite well the tune of "a little help from my friends, or a lending institution will do." Or maybe the business of stock shares amazes you, so you decide to buy or sell shares, which could benefit all involved, to swing monies over your way. Of course the B.S. line is never excluded in making deals—but not advised.

Help is definitely a fact of life. There's no way under the sun to avoid it or get around it. Every day of your life there will be some factor affecting you, whether good or bad where you're found giving or taking some service or help.

That dream house you've been planning on for quite some time will still crease your bank account, so why not get a loan to help. You high school graduates who strive for higher education will seek a bank loan or scholarship to push your plans through. That's help! Help is universal and definitely a part of this life. Are you ashamed? well, don't be. A fool is one who needs help and won't take help. A winner is one who needs help, takes help and uses help to help himself. Did I lose you there for a moment? Hope not. Just stressing a little common knowledge here and there. Take help. It's nothing to be ashamed of. Remember this and you won't ever feel guilty again. Everybody uses help constantly to get what they want!

Now, it's on you, alone, from here on out but do remember something will you? Don't give up. This message is for those of you who feel you are ugly ducklings and lost before you even get started, because you look at yourself as just plain ugly. Well, one thing for sure, you can't alter your looks too much and all the plastic surgery in the world can't make you look the identical same way you were in the beginning. Don't worry about it. Don't let it get you down. All God's creations are beautiful. Your day will come.

Now who the hell says it can't be done!!

X

Human Behavior

Human behavior is in a field all alone. The human race is categorized as most intelligent species of animals inhabiting the planet earth. But there are still many of us today who, by choice or pressure, invade the country's insane asylums as patients daily. This breakdown in human behavior comes about through matters of the mind. The difference between the happy people and the unhappy is a result of their level of thinking, and one thin line. All the money in the world can't bring happiness, which many already know, so we will deal mainly here with human behavior.

A great part of self-fulfillment in life is to have happiness and since the happiness of people begins with accepting, not searching, then you must first of all set up personal standards for yourself. Do not waste foolish time chasing after someone else's, because you run the high risk of walking on one thin line which you can fall off head first any time. That's not security. Security is knowing where your head is and following it. That's why the head is located at the top of the shoulders and not below the ankles. Its primary function is to think for you, not carry you. People who are contented in what they are doing at the present have fewer fears of the future and of growing old. Life has a meaning and direction to them, so these mental blocks are not present in this individual's life with respect to controlling the good things which he can make happen in his life. Maybe there is a sucker born every minute, but you're determined not to be a part of those statistics and who blames you. Even a sucker gets tired of playing the fool.

What makes people get sick and die is influenced a great deal more by daily habits than by illness and disease, as is documented into records today. For example, you're so tired of people telling you what to do with your life. Your lifestyle may not be their idea of a good life, but it is your life and that is all you have. All of it is yours. These people may tell you, be this way; be that way; live this way; live that way. Well, who knows any better than *you* whom you want to be. That's what's important—what *you* want, what *you* need.

Let's go to another example here. Some animals we use as pets show an excellent amount of intelligence. Take for instance the dog. Now the average house dog will acquire many of his owners' habits just through time and, like human beings, acquire habits which are accepted by the family. Children are basically naughty and so is a puppy dog. You can find the most disciplined child—then somewhere along the line, there's a dog the same way. A mentally disturbed child—a dog the same way. Just as this child may cause harm to himself or others around him, so can a dog who goes around biting any and everybody. Just remember that somewhere in this world there is something to match your image.

Take for instance the television, which creates a strong influence on the development of especially young minds (and old ones too for that matter). The picture can be found in ten out of ten American homes today. Movies are a prime example of the following: Have you ever been walking somewhere for the very first time in your life and enter into a scene that you know is your very first time of viewing it but in the back of your mind it seems a familiar place? Somehow you can't place this location. You can't tie it in. Well, don't be alarmed because it will happen to all of us sometime along life's trail. Everyone of us has been somewhere before in a dream. But my God, it seems so real! Now we're back into dealing with the mind.

I went to a movie once and left a complete wreck. My nerves had been worked over so badly that it took me several hours for reorganization again. That movie made such a dramatic impact on my mind until hibernation was the best thing to do. It just so happened the movie was shown on a Thursday night and the next morning, I sent a message of sudden sickness by a dear friend (bless her heart), to classes Friday morning to excuse me for cutting class that day. This was the only class I had the whole semester that required full attendance—three days a week. What a drag. Anyway, I managed to stretch my hibernation period into Sunday, which gave me plenty of time to reorganize my head through the weekend. Remember what I said earlier? Reorganization results in the ultimate purpose, that of rebuilding. There was no night life for me because I was too paranoid. This behavior took place during my college days. The movie was concerning the morbid world of life after death associated with the supernatural.

Television thrillers are the chill coolers when shown at night and this is why they have the better effect on the mind. After you've finished watching an excellent horror movie, a pin could drop and you most likely will hear it. You're jittery and off-balance for awhile. But that movie did take you away in its command for awhile or did it not. If it did not, then you would not have been shaken by its temporary impact. You see it wasn't the movie at all, but the mind and how it reacted to the story. That all has to do with social conditioning and social exposure. That's just like forcing an owl to sit out in the sun all day. The old spook would burn to death from a sun stroke. Everyone has a fear of some kind, no matter what age group he falls in. If you will notice, fear always comes from dealings with the unknown—things, angles, options which are all different, which are never the same. The next time you don't understand something, arrange your perception toward another angle, then pursue another option when that first one falls short. Repeat this process until you score.

The mind is a terrible thing to waste and all the money in the world can't replace one, but still there are countless lost souls out there, who are falling off, every day, into something they don't know how the hell to get out of. It can happen to everyone at least once in a lifetime—how about that!

Life is based on time, so we are safe to say all things end in time. But who is to say how long your time will last here on earth? For some life ends at infancy, babies who were only here a little while. Then there's the old-timer, who made it to a full and rich life. But what about that group in between? Some won't be fortunate enough to see their twenties. Then some twenties won't see their thirties. Some thirties won't reach their forties. Many forties are experiencing a change of life, if you happen to be female, and won't see their fifties. If you do reach fifty you'll be half-way there and can begin to look back at that life of yours.

At fifty, you're beginning to slow down that jet set life of yours if not before. Your children may be up in age now, so you can now take it slower. Sixty begins to creep in there. You're taking it really cautious and thankful to the good Lord he blessed you once again. Seventy—you made it! The good old ripe age. Now anything could start happening, and, oddly enough, you may now be ready for anything. Seventy—your wonderful, rich, golden age.

Many folks will stand up and say they are not yet ready to go at any age, but we all will go someday. When you get to go you're going, its unexpected for some and common knowledge to others. Enjoy your life while you can now, because one thing for sure is it will end one day forever and, if you did not do all the things ever dreamed of doing, or for that matter even half the things you wanted to do, you will leave this life miserable as hell. Now tell me, is that any way to go!

Are you doing your thing yet? Start today, because tomorrow is not promised to anyone. Your life is programmed before you're born up until that last breath of air. Everybody is a superstar because:

1. you know who you are
2. what you are
3. what you want
4. and last and most important what you have to do to hold it tight

Live, people, live because it has nothing to do with whether tomorrow will come. Anyway, who's complaining. We all go together! PEACE to you and yours forever.

> *Yesterday is history*
>
> *Tomorrow is your future*
>
> *Today is your beginning*
>
> *Use it wisely to reach tomorrow*
>   —BEVERLY BETHEA GRIFFIN SHIPPY

Glossary

Abstract—extreme
Acquire—characters that are a result of the environment
Anodyze—medication given for pain
Book—to run away from, exit
B.S.—bull shit
Clean House—unanimous sweep
Cleave—clever
Earthlin's—human occupants of the planet earth
Fuse—blow, entertain
Gigs—jobs
Grove—enjoy, get into
Headstrong—unyielding
Hideous—horrible and frightful to one's senses
Hip—to inform, up-dated news
Hit On—to direct comments toward, to discuss
Instruments—devices
Invading—to enter
Jinxie—a thing, person or situation guaranteed to bring with it
   bad luck
Knot Holes—legal loop holes
Light—absent-minded, dumb
Liquidation—dissolving of a marriage
Longwinded—articulate smoothly and at length
Nonchalant—practical, cool, unconcerned
Piece—book, novel, manuscripts
Place—to climb, to reach goal
Play—action

Ripoffs—substantially high prices
Schooled—well educated, informed, briefed in advance
Splurging—overspending
Tee—target
Universal—international, worldwide
Uptight—wound up
Well Doer—financially stable
: , " ! % ?—stressful points